COMMAND BLOCKS

HACKS FOR MINECRAFTERS

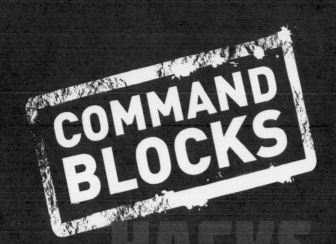

COMMAND BLOCKS

HACKS FOR MINECRAFTERS

THE UNOFFICIAL GUIDE TO TIPS AND TRICKS THAT OTHER GUIDES WON'T TEACH YOU

MEGAN MILLER
with ANTHONY HEDDINGS

Sky Pony Press
New York

Copyright © 2015, 2019 by Hollan Publishing, Inc.

First trade paperback edition 2019.

Minecraft® is a registered trademark of Notch Development AB.

The Minecraft game is copyright © Mojang AB.

Sky Pony Press books may be purchased in bulk at special discounts for sales promotion, corporate gifts, fund-raising, or educational purposes. Special editions can also be created to specifications. For details, contact the Special Sales Department, Sky Pony Press, 307 West 36th Street, 11th Floor, New York, NY 10018 or info@skyhorsepublishing.com.

Sky Pony® is a registered trademark of Skyhorse Publishing, Inc.®, a Delaware corporation.

Minecraft® is a registered trademark of Notch Development AB.
The Minecraft game is copyright © Mojang AB.

Visit our website at www.skyponypress.com.

10 9 8 7 6 5 4 3 2 1

Library of Congress Cataloging-in-Publication Data is available on file.

Print ISBN: 978-1-5107-4107-2
Ebook ISBN: 978-1-5107-4126-3

Printed in China

TABLE OF CONTENTS

COMMAND BLOCKS

HACKS FOR MINECRAFTERS

INTRODUCTION

Welcome to the slightly crazy world of commands and command blocks. With commands, you can do all kinds of things that aren't possible in a regular Survival world. You can create a super-powerful zombie or a villager that will trade diamonds for dirt, build towers of emerald blocks, and instantly teleport to any location.

This book will show you how commands work, and it will look at the most popular commands for creating fun creatures and effects, whether playing by yourself or creating a map for others to play. You'll also see how you can use command blocks to create commands that anyone in your multiplayer world can use.

There's no undo button in Minecraft.

Commands are very powerful, and some can change your world significantly. Remember that there's no undo button in Minecraft. As you are starting to use and understand commands and how they work, use a test world that you won't mind losing if disaster strikes. I've included instructions for creating a test world in the first chapter.

Lastly, some commands are a little different in varying versions of Minecraft. This book covers the command system for Java Edition 1.13. It doesn't cover commands used for managing users on a server. Commands used in the scoreboard system used to create complicated, custom gameplay are listed, but not explained, as this mechanic is out of the reach of this title.

CHAPTER 1

WHAT IS A COMMAND?

A command, in Minecraft and many other computer programs, is a string of very specific words that the software is programmed to react to. Some commands in Minecraft give you items you wouldn't normally get playing a game in Survival mode, so these are sometimes called cheats.

For example, you can use the /experience (/xp in BE) command to give a player any amount of experience points (XP). That's pretty cheaty, but in a special mini-game, giving XP can be a great reward to players who have accomplished some specific feat.

There are commands for doing all different types of things in Minecraft. Some commands are used only by an operator, or op, for managing, allowing, and banning players on the server. These commands aren't available to use in command blocks. Other commands can only be used on players (like giving them XP) or on blocks (like putting a block at a specific location). There are also commands that affect the whole world, like changing it to nighttime or daytime. We'll look at these different types of commands (except for the server management commands) and how to use them in the following chapters.

NOTE: To use commands in a single-player world, you must either be playing in Creative mode or have created your world with cheats on. If you are playing on multiplayer, you must be a server administrator or operator (op).

You use commands in Minecraft in the chat window. For example, to give yourself 30 XP levels, you open the chat window by pressing T. (You can also open the chat window by pressing /, and this will enter the first / of the command for you.) Then type:

```
/experience add [yourIGN] 30 levels
```

As you type, you'll notice that the game makes suggestions to complete your command. You can press Tab to accept and enter a suggestion.

When you type a command, the chat interface will suggest the correct spelling of the command and variables. It will also show you (in red) where you made an error if you enter a command incorrectly.

Other commands are more complicated, and you must include ID numbers or names and codes that reference specific traits or other variables. For example, to create a tame black horse with white spots, a couple blocks away from you and wearing a saddle, you would type:

```
/summon minecraft:horse ~ ~1 ~ {Variant:772,
ArmorItem:{id:diamond_horse_armor},
SaddleItem:{id:saddle,Count:1},Age:0,Tame:1}
```

To summon a tame horse with a specific color, markings, and a saddle takes a much longer command than granting someone XP.

The next chapter, Command Rules (or Syntax), will look at all the various parts of a command and how you put a command together.

Setting Up a New World

If you are playing and practicing with commands and command blocks, it can be helpful to set up a Superflat Creative world. The Superflat world is . . . super flat! There are no mountains, ravines, or rivers that can make it difficult to set up special areas or to concentrate on building. The default Superflat world however only has a few layers of blocks. This means that ground level is lower than y=40. And that means you could have tons of slimes spawning and interfering with you! This superflat world adds enough levels in so this won't happen.

To set up a new single-player Superflat Creative world to use for playing with command blocks:

1. Start Minecraft, or quit your current game, so that you are at the opening Minecraft screen. Choose Singleplayer to open up the Select World screen.

2. On the Select World screen, click Create New World.

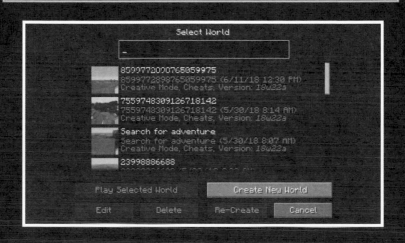

3. In the Create New World screen, type in the name of your world (this could be something descriptive, like Command Block World) Click the Game Mode button until it says Game Mode Creative. Click More World Options.

4. In the World Options screen, click the World Type button until it reads "Superflat" and then click the Customize button that appears.

Create New World

Seed for the world generator

Leave blank for a random seed

Generate Structures: ON   World Type: Superflat

Villages, dungeons etc   Customize

Allow Cheats: OFF   Bonus Chest: OFF

Commands like /gamemode, /experience

Done

Create New World   Cancel

5. In the Superflat customization screen, click Presets to open the Select a Preset screen.

Superflat Customization

Layer Material	Height
Grass Block	Top – 1
Dirt	2
Bedrock	Bottom – 1

Remove Layer   Presets

Done   Cancel

6. In the Select a Preset screen that opens, type the following into the top text box. (You may be able to correct the type that is already there, or just delete any existing text.) The command below sets the biome to Jungle, which has a nice bright green grass! You could type in Plains or another biome instead if you like.

```
minecraft:bedrock,62*minecraft:dirt,
minecraft:grass_block;minecraft:jungle
```

Select a Preset

Want to share your preset with someone? Use the below box!

edrock,62*minecraft:dirt,minecraft:grass_block;minecraft:jungle_

Alternatively, here's some we made earlier!

Classic Flat

Tunnelers' Dream

Water World

Overworld

Snowy Kingdom

Use Preset   Cancel

7. Click Use Preset. In the Customization screen that displays again, you should see that the layers for your world are 1 grass at the top, 62 dirt in the middle, and 1 bedrock at the bottom.

Superflat Customization

Layer Material	Height
Grass Block	Top − 1
Dirt	62
Bedrock	Bottom − 1

Remove Layer	Presets
Done	Cancel

8. Click Done to exit the Customization screen.
9. Click Done to exit the World Options screen.
10. Click Create New World to create your command block world.

CHAPTER 2

COMMAND RULES (OR SYNTAX)

For a command to work, you have to use only the proper words for that command, and these words must be in a specific order. These rules for how you type a command are called syntax. Each Minecraft command has a syntax that you must follow. (If you don't, the command may not work or may do something unexpected.)

Basically, you type the name of the command, followed by parameters. Parameters are words or numerical values that specify more about who, what, and where the command acts on. You may also hear these words referred to as *specifiers*.

The syntax for a command describes what words and parameters belong in the command and in what order they should be typed, along with the spaces and punctuation needed between words.

For example, the syntax for the /summon command is:

```
/summon <EntityName> [x] [y] [z] [dataTag]
```

This means that the summon command must start with a slash and the word summon. After one space (the spaces are important!) it must be followed by an entity name. You can also add coordinates in the XYZ format to indicate the location at which to create the entity. Finally, you can add additional data tags for more attributes of the entity.

You don't have to type in values for every parameter. The syntax is written in a way that makes it clear what you do have to type and what is optional:

> **Regular text** = You must type anything in regular (not italic or slanting) text.
>
> *Italic text* = Parameters you replace with your own values
>
> **<Angle brackets>** = Parameters you must replace. Don't include the angle brackets.
>
> **[Square brackets]** = Parameters you don't have to replace. Don't include the square brackets.
>
> **optionA|optionB** = You must choose one out of the options shown.

IMPORTANT: Although you can omit parameters that are in square brackets, you must type in values for all parameters that are located before any used parameter. This is the only way the software knows what values belong to which parameter. In other words, once you omit a parameter, you can't include any parameters after this.

Look at this simple way to use the /summon command.

```
/summon villager
```

The command begins with a slash (/). Any commands you type in a chat window have to start with a slash. If you're using a command block, you leave the slash out.

Notice there are only two words: the command name and one parameter—the required parameter, EntityName. Both of these are typed in regular text in the syntax (on page 11), so you know they are necessary. But you don't type the parameter name EntityName. In the syntax, this was typed in italics, so you just replace the parameter with the actual value you want. (When you replace a parameter with the value you want, the value is often called the argument.) Here, you must type the official entity ID that Minecraft assigned to the entity you want. This command is for a villager, so I used the villager's entity ID name, which is villager.

This simple command doesn't list any specific traits or career the villager should have, or where the villager should appear. So this command creates a random villager at the default location, which is wherever you (or a command block) are located in the world.

A More Complicated Example Command

A more complex version of the /summon command is:

```
/summon villager 50 63 20 {CustomName:
"\"Fred\"",Profession:3,Career:3}
```

This command adds more parameters after the entity name Villager:

- **340 69 -220** These three numbers specify the XYZ coordinates to spawn the villager at. (And unless you're near that location, you won't see this villager being created!) Notice how these are typed with spaces in between. We'll go over how to use coordinates in commands and command blocks.

- **CustomName:"\"Fred\""** This is a data tag that changes the name of the villager to Fred. The set of data tags starts with a curly bracket. The \ that appears is called an escape character that tells the program that the characters that follow are literal characters. You'll use escape characters often for words that will be printed or shown on screen. For now, you need to know that these characters shown before and after Fred need to be used with the name you use for a CustomName. The next chapter looks at how you use and format these data tags properly.

- **Profession:Profession:3,Career:3** This data tag says the villager's career should be Profession 3 (Blacksmith) and Career 3 (Tool Smith).

You can add a custom name to almost everything in Minecaft. This villager's custom name was added with the entity dataTag "CustomName".

Specifying Blocks, Entities, and Items

So if you have the syntax of a command, how do you know what values you can use for the parameters? What can you use for EntityName, besides Villager? We'll go over what your options are with each command we look at.

Pretty much each type of "thing" in Minecraft, from creepers to diamond ore to chests, falls into one of three main categories: blocks, items, and entities. Each object has a special ID name that you use in commands to specify that object.

Almost all objects in Minecraft are categorized into three main categories: blocks (left), items (middle), and entities (right).

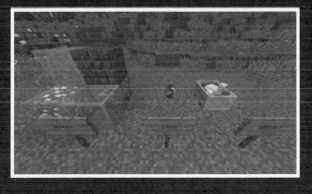

The appendices at the back of this book list many of these objects and their ID names. This means that when you look at a command syntax that asks for an <Item>, you can look in the Item ID appendix to find the ID name for the item you want. When a command syntax asks you to use a Block ID, you can look in the Block ID appendix.

It's very important to type a command with no spelling, spacing, punctuation, capitalization, or other typing errors (typos).

If you don't, the command will either fail or give you unexpected results. For example, you could accidentally type in the wrong world coordinates to which to teleport a player. Wrong coordinates can lead to burning in a lava pool or suffocating inside an extreme hill!

If you type a command incorrectly you will get a fail message. If you type it correctly, you will get a success message even if you use wrong information, like the wrong coordinates. So a success message doesn't always mean the command worked the way you wanted it to.

If your Minecraft chat window gets too busy with notices and announcements, you can clear it by pressing F3 and D.

When you are typing commands, try to think of each word not as a whole word but as a string of foreign characters. You have to look at every character, including spaces, to make sure it is the right one and is in the right order. One character missing is a fail, because programs like games aren't built to autocorrect spelling and punctuation.

Minecraft's autocomplete feature is a huge help in typing commands and spelling ID names and terms correctly. As soon as you type / in the chat window the auto-complete feature is ready. First, after the slash, press Tab to see a list of possible commands.

Here I've typed in the / to start a command and pressed Tab to show a list of available commands.

You can also type in the first letter or letters of a command, to see a list of commands that begin with those letters.

Press Tab a second time to move the cursor to the end of the command name. Then, you can use Tab (or the up and down arrow keys) to cycle through the list options. Finally, when the command you want is selected and shown in your text box, you can press Space to enter the command and move to the next word.

At this point, once you've entered the space to move to the next word, you can press Esc to show the syntax for the command. (Don't press it twice, or you'll be ejected from chat!) Even without pressing Esc, as you type the command, the autocomplete feature will give tips as to what parameters are expected next in the sequence.

Press Esc after you've entered a space to view the command's syntax. Also notice in the text above, the fail or error messages in red. These include a pointer showing at what point in the command the error occurs. In white is a typical success message, confirming what the command did.

After pressing the space that moves you on to the next word after the command, Minecraft will show a valid parameter for your command or list of valid parameters. Press Tab to move the cursor to the end of the word and then press Tab again to move through the choices. When the one you want is selected, press Space to enter it. The autocomplete will help you through all of the parameters the command uses.

Finally, at the end of the command, Minecraft may show you an option for entering data tags, with the prompt: [<nbt>]. Notice that it is enclosed in square brackets, which means these extra data tags aren't required. Entering a valid data tag is a bit trickier than Autocomplete can help with, so we'll look at this in Chapter 3.

Once you've typed in your command, make sure the command has no red text, which indicates an error, then press Enter to execute the command.

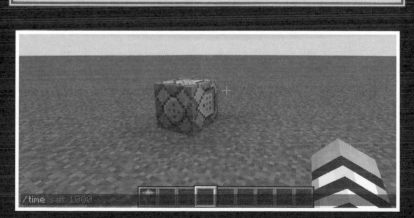

Red text in your command indicates an error. The error location is at the first appearance of red text. Even if other parts of the command are correct, everything after the error will be shown in red.

give @p minecraft:command_block 20

A finished, successful command show different parts of the command in different colors. Here, the command is gray, the target selector value (@p) is light blue, the required argument for item (command_block) is yellow, and the entry for the count is green.

Get Outside Help!

There are lots of command generators online that you can use to help you with your command. They have a form you fill out to select commands, parameters, and arguments. When you are finished, you usually click a button, and a text box will show you your finished command. Copy (Ctrl/Command+C) this text, go to Minecraft, and paste (Ctrl/Command+V) this copied command into the chat window or into a command block. With online generators, you do need to make sure that the generator works with your version of Minecraft.

Two online generators are:

https://www.digminecraft.com/generators/
http://minecraft.tools

CHAPTER 3

CUSTOMIZING COMMANDS

In Chapter 2, you saw how parameters are used with commands. Choosing values (or arguments) for some parameters is fairly simple, like choosing a Block Name. Others, like <X Y Z>, target selectors, and <dataTag>, are a bit more complex. There are a number of ways to use values for these.

XYZ Coordinates

The XYZ coordinates that you use in a command show the exact place in the world at which the command should take place or create something, along imaginary lines called axes. When you use XYZ coordinates, there's always an imaginary center at 0 0 0. In Minecraft, 0 0 0 is set to be around your original spawn point.

The Debug screen shows you the coordinates where you are standing, the block you are standing on, and the block you are looking at.

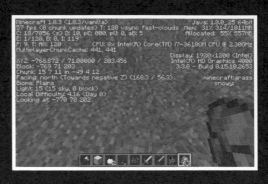

- **X:** Where you are on an east–west (X) line or axis. This number is negative when the location is west of the center.

- **Y:** Where you are on a vertical axis. This number is negative when the location is below the center.

- **Z:** Where you are on a north–south axis. This is negative when the location is north of the center.

The X-axis (red) shows where you are on an east–west imaginary line. The Y-axis (green) shows you where you are vertically. The Z-axis (blue) shows you where you are along a north–south line.

To find a coordinate, open up your debug screen by pressing 3. Look for these entries in the bottom left section

- **XYZ:** This entry shows exactly where you are standing, with decimals.

- **Block:** This shows the XYZ coordinates for the block you are standing on.

- **Facing:** This shows which way you are looking.
- **Looking at:** This shows what block your cursor is pointing at. This entry only shows up when you are close enough to a block that it shows a thin line around it.

So when you need to enter a real XYZ coordinate for a command, you can go to the location you want it to appear. If you want it to appear above the block you are standing on or looking at, you'll have to add 1 for each block you are raising the location.

Relative Coordinates

You can also use relative locations. These say where the XYZ location should be in relation to where the command was given. This is either where you are when you enter the command in chat or where the command block is.

You specify an XYZ location with a tilde (~). The key for this squiggly line is usually at the top left of your keyboard. You use three tildes by themselves, in place of the XYZ coordinates, to set the location at the command-giver's location. You can also type a number, positive or negative, after any tilde to specify the distance in blocks, along that axis, away from the command-giver's location.

~ ~ ~: This makes command execute at the location of the command-giver.

~1 ~ ~-2: In this example, the X is ~1. This says the command must execute 1 block east (because it is a positive number) of the command-giver. The Y is the tilde by itself. So this says to execute the command at the same vertical (Y) position as the command-giver. Finally, the ~-2 for the Z position says that the command should execute 2 blocks north (because it is a negative number) of the command-giver's location. For example, to summon a villager two blocks north from you, you would use:

```
/summon villager ~ ~ ~-2
```

Use the Debug screen (F3) to find coordinates for the block you are standing on and a block you are looking at.

Local Coordinates

Local coordinates are similar to relative coordinates. Like relative coordinates, they are measured from the entity issuing the command. Unlike relative coordinates, local coordinates take into account the way the entity is facing. The three directions are left, up and forwards, and local coordinates are identified with a caret (^) instead of a tilde (~). So to summon a villager 3 blocks in front of you, you would use the command

```
/summon villager ^ ^1 ^3.
```

Target Selectors

Some commands allow you to use target selectors. Target selectors let you select one or more players or entities without knowing their exact locations or names. You use a special target variable instead of a name or ID.

@p   This selects the nearest person to the command-giver.

@r   This selects a random player in the world.

@a   This selects all players in the world.

@e   This selects all entities in the world (including players).

@s   This selects the entity issuing the command.

You can also be more specific by using arguments with a target selector. For example, you could limit entities targeted to endermen with:

`@e[type=enderman]`

With target selectors, you have to use argument:value pairs. These argument:value pair or pairs have to be enclosed in square brackets. If there's more than one pair, you use a comma with no space to separate the pairs. For example, to teleport any creepers that are between 1 and 64 blocks from you to a random player, you would type:

`/teleport @e[type=creeper,distance=1..64] @r`

Common Target Selectors

Type	Argument	Description and Example
Location (Coordinates)	x, y, z	Selects targets only at these absolute coordinates. `@p[x=12,y=63,z=40]`
Location (Distance)	distance	Selects targets at a specific distance from the command issuer. You can include a range by using two periods after the smaller number. You can leave a range open ended (at either end) by omitting the furthest or nearest distance. `@e[distance=10]` `@e[distance=10..20]` `@e[distance=10..]` `@e[distance=..20]`

Location (Volume)	dx, dy, dz	Selects targets within a volume--an imaginary box of space. The box is dx wide along the x axis, dz long along the z axis, and dy high along the y axis. It has a northwest corner at the location the command was executed. If xyz coordinates are also specified, then that will be the volume's corner. `@e[dx=20,dy=10,dz=20]`
Entity Type	type	Select targets by entity type. `@e[type=creeper]` Can also use a NOT qualifier by placing an exclamation point in front of the value. This example will select only entities that aren't creepers. `@e[type=!creeper]`
Experience Level	level	Select targets by experience level. This can also use ranges. `@p[level=10]` `@p[level=10..20]`
Game mode	game-mode	Select players playing in a specific game mode. Values are survival, creative, adventure, spectator. Can also use NOT (!) qualifier. `@p[gamemode=survival]` `@p[gamemode=!creative]`
Limit	limit	Restricts the number of possible targets to a limit. `@p[limit=12]` Possible targets can also be sorted with the sort argument. Values can be nearest, furthest, random, arbitrary. `@p[limit=12,sort=nearest]`

Name	name	Select targets by name. Can also use NOT (!) qualifier. If the name has spaces in it, use quotation marks around the name.

		`@p [name=Fred]`
		 `@p [name=!Fred]`
		 `@p [name="Big Fred"]`

Working with Data Tags

Some advanced or complicated commands can have long strings of data tag parameters in them. These data tags help define the traits or properties of items, blocks, and entities. Data tags are grouped and enclosed in either square or curly brackets:

[List Tags]: Tags that are lists, or can have several values separated by commas, use square brackets. The square brackets let the computer software know that what follows is a list, and commas separate each different value.

{Compound Tags}: Tags that are defined as "compound tags" use curly brackets. A compound tag has an identifying parameter name, such as "id", followed by a colon ":", followed by a space and then the value "1". The curly brackets let the computer software know to expect this type of information and when it ends.

Data Tags and Data Values

Data tags are different from data values. Data tags are attribute: value pairs that describe various characteristics of an item or entity. The attribute is the type of characteristic, like a custom name. A value specifies what the name actually is.

Here's an example of a very long command that gives the nearest player a chest with a couple of items in it:

```
/give @p chest{BlockEntityTag:{Items:[{Slot:0,
id:white_wool,Count:4},{Slot:1,id:obsidian,
Count:8},{Slot:2,id:diamond_sword,Count:1}]}} 1
```

Chest{ This specifies a chest to be given, and the opening bracket indicates that a compound data tag follows.

BlockEntityTag:{ This is an NBT tag used for tile entities (also called block entities). Blocks that have special functions beyond being ordinary blocks are actually categorized as tile entities, such as chests, brewing stands, and beacons. Chests have block entity data that includes "items", and you can define items for slots 0-26 for a chest. The opening bracket shows that more compound tags that identify attributes of the chest will follow.

Items:[This opens a list of tags that will be the items inside the chest. Each item is identified by the slot it fits into, the type of item, and the number of that item. In the first slot, 0, will be four white wool blocks, in the second, 8 obsidian, and in the third, 1 diamond sword.

The data tags that you can use for different entities and items depend on that object. The Minecraft Wiki has a long list of what data tags (also called NBT tags) work with what item or entity, at http://minecraft.gamepedia.com/Chunk_format, under the heading NBT Structure.

Entities (including players) especially can have many many data tags that define them: Where they are facing, if they have an effect on them, if they can take damage, and many more. The commands used in this book will show some data tags, but not all. You can find the full lists of data tags for an entity on the official Minecraft Wiki (minecraft.gamepedia.com.) Here you can search for an entity, like Villager. On the Villager page, you'll find a list of data tags and values you can use when you summon a villager.

Balancing Brackets

It is very important to make sure each opening bracket has a closing bracket to match it, at the right place. It is also incredibly easy to forget a bracket. Autocomplete will highlight an unpaired bracket in red. Simple code editing software, like Atom for Mac or Notepad++ for Windows, can help highlight brackets that match or are missing. You can also use a regular text editor (TextEdit in Mac or Notepad in Windows) to write out long commands in a way that shows where the brackets are, so you can make sure they are balanced. When you're done fixing bracket problems, you can remove the breaks before and after brackets to keep the command on one line as usual.

```
/give @p chest
  { BlockEntityTag:
    {Items:
     [
       {Slot:0,id:white_wool,Count:4},
       {Slot:1,id:obsidian,Count:8},
       {Slot:2,id:diamond_sword,Count:1}
     ]
    }
  } 1
```

CHAPTER 4

USING COMMAND BLOCKS

Command blocks are blocks that you place in the Minecraft world. Each command block can have one command assigned to it. To execute the command, you activate the block by sending it a redstone signal. The simplest way to do this is to place a button on the actual command block.

Differences between Command Blocks and Chat Commands

- Command blocks can take very long commands, while Chat entries are limited to 100 characters.

- Players without op status can execute commands in command blocks. (Only ops can place commands in command boxes, though.)

- Command blocks are much more powerful than Chat commands since you can control them with redstone.

- Two or more commands can be linked together by linking command blocks with redstone or using chain command blocks.

- Using relative coordinates in a command block means the location will be relative to the command block, not where you are.

Getting Command Blocks

Command blocks are very powerful, so they aren't available by crafting or in the Creative inventory. You have to use a command in the Chat window to get them. To give yourself a stack of 64 command blocks, type the following into the chat window:

```
/give  @p  minecraft:command_block 64
```

Adding Commands to Command Blocks

You must be in Creative mode to add commands to command blocks. To assign a command to a command block:

1. Place the block on the ground where you want it to be. Remember that its location will determine where any relative coordinates point to.

2. Right-click the command block to open the command block interface.

3. Type (or paste) the command into the Console Command text box. (The box below is where the command block shows success or error messages for the last executed command. You can turn this off by clicking the button 0 to make it X.)

4. Click Done to assign the command and close the interface.

You type a command into the Console Command text box at the top of the command block interface.

Types of Command Blocks

There are three different kinds of command blocks. The default command block is orange and is called an Impulse command block. Impulse command blocks execute their commands only when they receive redstone signal.

If you place down an Impulse command block, you can change its type by right-clicking it to open the interface and clicking on the button that says "Impulse".

The other two types of command blocks are Repeat and Chain. Repeat command blocks will execute their command every tick (20 times a second!). This is useful if you want a command to always be running.

Be careful with what commands you put into Repeat command blocks! If you put a /give command, your inventory would quickly fill up!

Here's a fun command to try with Repeat command blocks. Grab a few snowballs and a few boats, and put this command into a repeat command block:

```
/execute @e[type=Snowball] ~ ~-4 ~ /fill ~-2
~ ~-2 ~2 ~ ~2 minecraft:water 0 replace air
```

Make sure to click the "Needs Redstone" button to change it to "Always Active". This command will make a pool of water below every snowball you throw! It can get out of hand pretty quick, but it's fun to ride around on the towers of water with a boat.

You might see your chat fill up with messages from command blocks. To turn this off, run:

```
/gamerulecommandBlockOutput false
```

WARNING: Using a Repeat command block to loop a command over and over again can use up too much memory and can crash your game or machine. When you are experimenting, use a test world that you don't mind losing if something goes wrong, or make a backup of your world.

The other type of command block is Chain. Chain command blocks are placed in a line, and when the first one in the line is activated, the next one activates, going down the line in order. This is useful for making chains or commands that need to be in order.

Activating and Linking Command Blocks

To activate an Impulse command block, you have to send it a redstone signal. While redstone is too big a topic to cover in this book, there are simple solutions for activating command blocks. You basically just need to attach a power source to the block and turn it on. For example:

1. Place a button or lever on the block. You will need to hold shift while right-clicking to do this. The lever has two positions, on and off, so you click it once to turn the signal on. Then, to repeat the command, you have to turn it off, and then back on again. The button automatically turns itself off, so each time you press it the block will execute the command. Make sure the command block is on Impulse, not Repeat!

2. Place a button or lever on another non-transparent block, and connect that block to the command block with redstone dust. The line of redstone dust must point directly at the command block.

Combining Command Blocks

You can connect command blocks in a line by setting the command blocks to Conditional. A Conditional command block will only run its command if the block behind it ran its command with no errors. They're a lot like Chain command blocks, except Chain command blocks don't check if a command failed or not, and you can use Repeat command blocks in the conditional chain as well.

You can also combine command blocks to the outside world with a redstone signal that links to each one, with redstone dust and/or redstone repeaters. A redstone repeater needs to face into the command block to send it a signal.

You can activate several command blocks at the same time by connecting them all to a single button, lever, or other power source.

TIP: It can be easy to forget what a command block does. Add a sign next to your command blocks that reminds you what each of them does.

CHAPTER 5

BASIC COMMANDS

Some commands are very simple, general commands. Some of these can be used by anyone, not just an op. Basic commands include:

/difficulty
/gamemode
/help
/list
/me
/say
/tell

The /difficulty Command

This command sets the difficulty level of the current game, which can be Peaceful, Easy, Normal, or Hard.

For example, you might use one command block to change your Normal Survival world to Peaceful, in order to kill all hostile mobs. When you are done playing in Peaceful, use a second command block to change the world back to Normal to set your game back to Survival mode. You can also connect these two command blocks with redstone, so that you first change to Peaceful to kill hostiles and then go immediately back to your Normal Survival mode.

Syntax

```
/difficulty <difficulty level>
```

- Replace <difficulty level> with one of the following:
    - peaceful
    - easy
    - normal
    - hard

Example

```
/difficulty peaceful
```

The /gamemode Command

This command changes a player's current gamemode to Survival, Creative, Adventure, or Spectator. (Hardcore isn't a true game mode—it combines Hard difficulty level with having only one life in a world.) This can be handy in a game map, where you want to change a player from Adventure mode to Spectator mode if they die (and are out of the game).

Syntax

```
/gamemode <mode> [player]
```

- Replace <mode> with one of the following:
  - survival
  - creative
  - adventure
  - spectator

- May replace [player] with the username of a single player or a target selector. If you don't specify a player, you will change your own game mode. If you are using this in a command block, you must specify a player.

Examples

```
/gamemode survival
/gamemode spectator
```

The /help Command

Any player can use the /help command to get information about commands. You can type /help for a list of all commands or get help for a specific command by typing the command name after help.

Syntax

```
/help [<command>]
```

- Replace <command> with the name of a command.

Example

```
/help give
```

The /list Command

Any player can use the /list command, which simply lists all the players that are currently playing. You can also press the Tab key for the same information.

Syntax

```
/list
```

The /me Command

Any player can use this command to send a message to other players. This "me" message always begins with your user name.

Syntax

```
/me <any text>
```

- Replace <any text> with the text of your choice. You can include target selectors, like @p.

Example

`/me makes sadface`

This displays as: *meganfair makes sadface.

Notice that the message display starts with an asterisk (*) before your username. This lets other players know that the message is coming from another player.

If you are an op, you can also use target selectors in the <any text> you include. This will result in one or more targets' usernames being displayed. Also, if you use this in a command block, the message displayed will replace "/me" with "@". @ is the default name of the command block, but you can rename a command block with an anvil. Then the /me command will use the command block's given name. So, if you name a command block "The Flying Spaghetti Monster" and have it execute this command, it will show in Chat as:

*The Flying Spaghetti Monster makes sadface.

The /say Command

The /say command sends a message in the chat screen to all players. This is almost identical to a chat message, but you can use target selectors like @p to include usernames in the message. If a command block is programmed with the /say command, it will use "@" as its display name. You can rename the command block with an anvil to change the command block's name. A second difference from a chat message is that the sayer's name is enclosed in square brackets, rather than the angled brackets used for names in Chat. You can use this with command blocks to give general announcements or make it seem like a message is coming from someone else—whatever you name the command block.

Syntax

`/say <any text>`

- Replace <any text> with your message.

Examples

`/say The server will shut down for maintenance at 5pm EST`

If I type this, the Chat will show:

[meganfair]The server will shut down for maintenance at 5pm EST

If a command block named "IMPORTANT" executes this, the Chat will show:

[IMPORTANT]The server will shut down for maintenance at 5pm EST

The /tell Command

Anyone can use the /tell command to send a private message to one or more players on the server. If an operator uses this command, he or she can use a target selector in place of usernames.

Syntax

```
/tell <player> <any text>
```

- Replace <player> with the username of the player you are sending the message to.
- Replace <any text> with your private message.

In place of tell, you can also use "w" (whisper) or "msg" (message).

Example

```
/tell BigRabbit Do you want to play Death Games?
```

If I send this message to player BigRabbit on my server, BigRabbit (and only BigRabbit) will see the following message:

meganfair whispers to you: Do you want to play Death Games?

CHAPTER 6

WORLD COMMANDS

World commands change something that affects the entire world or game. For example, the /weather command changes what the weather is, and the /time command changes what time it is in the game.

World commands include:

/defaultgamemode
/gamerule
/seed
/setworldspawn
/time
/toggledownfall
/weather
/worldborder

This command changes the game mode that new players on the server will be in: Survival, Creative, Adventure, or Spectator. You'd use this command on a multiplayer server, perhaps with an adventure map. You could use this command to make sure that every player that starts playing in the world is in Adventure mode, so that they can't break down buildings, for example.

In Spectator mode, you are invisible to other players. But if you press F5, you can see other players who are also in Spectator mode. You appear to each other as a transparent head floating around.

Syntax

`/defaultgamemode <mode>`

- Replace <mode> with one of the following arguments:
    - survival
    - creative
    - adventure
    - spectator

Example

`/defaultgamemode adventure`

The /gamerule Command

The /gamerule command lets you set basic game options for your world or find out the current game options. You can also create a new game rule that you can use to store a value that you can retrieve and use later. This would be useful if you are combining command blocks to make a command block program.

Syntax

`/gamerule <rulename> [value]`

- Replace <rulename> with one of the game rules listed below.

- May replace [value] with a valid value for the game rule you are setting. This will generally be either true, false, or a number. If you don't type a value for the rule here, then the response will tell you what the game rule is currently set to.

Gamerules*		
GameRule	**Description**	**Values**
commandBlockOutput	If true, command blocks notify administrators when they execute a command. The default value is true.	true or false
doDaylightCycle	This stops and starts the sun and moon moving. The default value is true. You might use this on a map where you want it to be daylight the entire day, so that fewer mobs spawn naturally.	true or false

GameRule	Description	Values
doMobLoot	This allows mobs to drop items when they are killed, like zombies dropping rotten flesh. The default value is true. Turning this off means you also won't get meat from passive mobs, so you'll have to be a vegetarian, too.	true or false
doMobSpawning	This decides whether mobs (including passive and neutral mobs) should naturally spawn. The default value is true. Mobs can still spawn from spawners if this is set to false.	true or false
keepInventory	If you change this to true, whenever someone dies, all their inventory will remain with them. The default value is false. You might turn this on in a special Survival mini-game, where players die constantly. This allows them to get back into the fight quickly with their sword or bow and arrow.	true or false

GameRule	Description	Values
mobGriefing	This allows mobs to destroy or change blocks, such as creepers blowing up the landscape or sheep "eating" grass blocks and turning them into dirt. It also allows mobs like villagers, Endermen, and zombies to pick up items. The default value is true.	true or false
naturalRegeneration	This lets players naturally get back health points, as long as their hunger bar is high enough. The default value is true.	true or false
showDeathMessages	This turns on and off messages displaying in Chat when a player dies. The default value is true.	true or false

*This list is a shortened version of the full list on the Minecraft Wiki, which you can find at http://minecraft.gamepedia.com/Commands#gamemode

Use the mobGriefing option to turn off damage from creepers and other block-changing mobs.

Example

```
/gamerule mobGriefing false
```

The /seed Command

The /seed command displays the number for the world seed. If you used regular words for your seed, such as "awesome new world", the seed is still displayed as a number. This is because when you type in letters for a seed, the letters are converted into numbers. The seed is what helps the Minecraft software create entirely different worlds with new terrain. If you know the seed for your world, you can share the number with someone else. He or she can play the same world using your seed (you do have to be using the same version of Minecraft). Knowing the seed number can also help you find things like slime chunks. There are several online slime chunk finders that will take your seed number and let you know what areas slimes will spawn in (besides swamps at night). One slime finder is at chunkbase.com. (A chunk is a 16x16x256 block section of the world, used in the game programming.)

The slime chunks in your world are based on your world seed number. Slime chunks are 16x16 areas where slime will spawn at any light level, and below y=40.

Syntax

```
/seed
```

There are no parameters or arguments for this command, just type /seed.

The /setworldspawn Command

The /setworldspawn command allows you to change the spawn location for your world. The spawn location is where new players appear and where you respawn when you die if you haven't slept in a bed somewhere. This can be helpful if the original world spawn is in an inhospitable area. If you've made a mini-game or adventure map, you may want players to start in a special location.

The /setworldspawn command lets you set the spawn for your world somewhere more convenient for you.

Syntax

```
/setworldspawn [x y z]
```

- May replace [x y z] with the coordinates you want. If you leave the command as /setworldspawn, then the location of the command block (or your location) will be set as spawn.

The /time command lets you change the time in your world to a specific time or to day or night. You can also use it to jump forward in time by a specific amount or find out how many ticks have gone by since midnight or the start of the world.

Time in Minecraft software is measured in ticks. There are 20 ticks in a second, so each tick lasts .05 of a second. Because a Minecraft full day/night cycle lasts 20 minutes in real time, this means there are a total of 24,000 ticks in a Minecraft day. From this, you can also determine that an in-game Minecraft hour lasts about 50 seconds in real time.

Syntax

`/time <add|query|set> <value>`

- Replace <add|query|set> with one of the three options: add, query, or set.
- For "add", replace <value> with the number of ticks you want to add to the time, from 1 to 2147483647. To add a Minecraft hour, add 1000 ticks, and to add a day, add 24000.
- For "query", replace <value> with either "gametime" or "daytime". Gametime will return the total number of ticks since your world started, and daytime will return the number of ticks since midnight.
- For "set", replace <value> with either a number of ticks (from 0 to 2147483647), or "day", or "night". Setting the time to 1000 sets the time to day, and setting it to 13000 makes it nighttime.

Examples

```
/time set day
/time set 13000
/time add 24000
/time query gametime
```

The /weather Command

You can use the /weather command to change the weather to clear, rain, or thunder. (If you are in a snowy biome, you'll get snow instead of rain. If you are in a desert biome, you won't see the rain, except at the borders to another biome.) The game will decide how long the weather will last. You can also set how long the weather should last before the game returns to its normal weather programming.

If you use the /weather rain command in the desert, you won't see any rain. But if you move just one block into another biome, it will be raining there.

Syntax

```
/weather <clear|rain|thunder> [number of
seconds]
```

- Replace <clear|rain|thunder> with one of the three options: clear, rain, or thunder.
- May replace [number of seconds] with a number from 1 to 1000000 to set how many seconds (in real time) the weather lasts.

Examples

```
/weather clear 1000000
/weather thunder
```

There are eight /worldborder commands. A world border is a boundary to the edge of a Minecraft world. World borders are used by mapmakers for special maps or for mini-games, like an Ultra Hardcore game. Sometimes regular multiplayer servers will use a world border at the start of a new map so that players build close together for a while and get to know each other. The world border is a square boundary, with its default center at 0,0, that limits players to play within it. This command refers to the length of the radius of the border (though the world border is a square). This is the distance from the center of the world border to one of the four side edges. World borders can also be set to grow or reduce in size. A static world border is aqua. An expanding border is green, and a contracting one is red.

If you accidentally create a world border, you can remove it by setting the worldborder to 30000000 (30 million).

/worldborder add

The /worldborder add command lets you increase the size of the current world border. You can also set how many seconds it will take to expand from the current border to the new border.

Syntax

```
/worldborder add <blocks>[seconds]
```

- Replace <blocks> with the number of blocks you are adding.

- Replace [seconds] with the number of seconds (in real time) the expansion should take.

Example

```
/worldborder add 100 3600
```

/worldborder center

The /worldborder center command lets you specify the center of the world border square. The default center is 0,0.

Syntax

```
/worldborder center <x><z>
```

- Replace <x> and <z> with the X and Z coordinates of the new center. Because world borders cover the whole height of the map, you do not need to set the Y coordinate.

Example

```
/worldborder center 100 -100
```

/worldborder damage amount

By default, a world border gives .2 points of damage to a player for each block the player goes beyond the border's buffer zone. This command allows you to specify how many damage points are given per block.

Syntax

```
/worldborder damage amount <damage points>
```

- Replace <damage points> with the number of damage points a player will be dealt for each block he or she goes beyond the buffer.

Example

```
/worldborder damage amount 1
```

/worldborder damage buffer

The default buffer zone for a world border is five blocks, and players aren't damaged until they get beyond this. This command lets you change how many blocks deep, or beyond the border, the buffer zone is.

Syntax

```
/worldborder damage buffer <blocks>
```

- Replace <blocks> with the new size, in blocks, of the buffer.

Example

```
/worldborder damage buffer 3
```

/worldborder get

The /worldborder get command displays the size of the world border.

Syntax

```
/worldborder get
```

There are no additional parameters for this command, you just type /worldborder get.

/worldborder set

The worldborder set command lets you create a world border with a specific size. You can also set how many seconds it takes for the border to grow or retreat to the new size.

Syntax

```
/worldborder set <blocks>[seconds]
```

- Replace <blocks> with the radius size you want. An entire side's length of the world border will be double this, so if you set a radius of 500, the new world border will make a play zone of 1000x1000.

- May replace [seconds] with the time, in seconds, that it will take the current world border to change to the new size. (An hour is 3600 seconds.)

Example

```
/worldborder set 500 7200
```

Minecraft warns players about the world border by turning their screen red if they get close.

/worldborder warning distance

A world border will by default give a player a visual warning—the screen tints red—when they are within 5 blocks. This command allows you to set a different warning distance.

Syntax

```
/worldborder warning distance <blocks>
```

- Replace <blocks> with the distance from the border, in blocks, that a player will be warned.

Example

```
/worldborder warning distance 15
```

/worldborder warning time

If a world border is decreasing, and will reach a player within 15 seconds, that player will receive a warning. This command allows you to change the 15-second world border warning time.

Syntax

```
/worldborder warning time <seconds>
```

- Replace <seconds> with the amount of warning time a player should get for an approaching world border.

Examples

```
/worldborder warning time 120
```

CHAPTER 7

BLOCK COMMANDS

Block commands act on blocks. Blocks include all of the square cubes you can place in the world, from acacia wood planks to zombie heads. They also include crafted objects that you can place, like ladders and anvils. Block commands include:

/clone
/fill
/replaceitem
/setblock

The /clone command lets you copy blocks in a 3D area to another area. This is a terrific command for making copies of something that was hard to build, like a house or a complicated wall. You do have to be careful in figuring out the coordinates. You have to choose two opposite corner blocks of the area you are copying. Then, when you clone the area, you choose just one block for the destination location. The block you choose will be the lowest northwest corner of the new location. You won't be able to rotate your copy or make it face a different direction. You are also limited to a total number of 4,096 blocks to clone.

Syntax

`/clone <x1 y1 z1> <x2 y2 z2> <x y z>`
`[maskMode] [cloneMode] [TileName]`

- Replace <x1 y1 z1> with the XYZ coordinates at one corner of the area you are copying.

- Replace <x2 y2 z2> with the XYZ coordinates of the opposite area you are copying.

- Replace <x y z> with the XYZ coordinates of the location destination. The block you choose will be the lowest northwest corner of your copied area.

- May replace [maskMode] with one of the following:

  - **filtered:** You use this with the [Tilename] parameter to say which type of block should be copied. So you could copy only stone blocks, for example.
  - **masked:** This copies only blocks that are not air blocks.
  - **replace:** This copies all blocks. This is the default maskMode.

- May replace [cloneMode] with one of the following:

  - **force:** This allows cloning to an overlapping area.
  - **move:** This will fill the original area you are cloning with air blocks.
  - **normal:** This is the default.

- If you are using the maskMode filtered, you must replace [TileName] with the ID name of the block type you want cloned.

The /clone command is a great way to make copies of buildings, like village houses, quickly.

Example

```
/clone -778 64 307 -774 68 310 -778 64 314
/clone -778 64 307 -774 68 310 ~2 ~ ~2
filtered normal sandstone
```

The /fill Command

With the /fill command, you select a three-dimensional area and fill it with the block of your choice!

Syntax

```
/fill <x1 y1 z1> <x2 y2 z2> <block>
[oldBlockHandling] [dataTag]
[replaceBlock] [replaceDataValue]
```

- Replace <x1 y1 z1> and <x2 y2 z2> with the two opposite corners of your area.

- Replace <block> with the ID name of the block you are using to fill the area.

- May replace [oldBlock Handling] with one of the following:

   - **destroy:** This makes the replaced blocks drop as if they were mined.
   - **hollow:** This replaces only the outside edges of the area with the new block and fills the interior with air blocks.
   - **keep:** This replaces only air blocks in the region with the new block.

- ○ **outline:** This is the same as hollow, except the interior blocks aren't changed.
- ○ **replace:** This is the default and replaces all blocks.

- May replace [dataTag] with a data tag for the new block. You cannot use this if you are using [replaceTileName] or [replaceDataValue].

- May replace [replaceBlock] with the type of block to replace in the region. This means, for example, that you can specify only to replace stone brick blocks with cobblestone blocks. This works only when you are using the oldBlockHandling value replace.

- May replace [replaceDataValue] with the data value of the block to be replaced. This works only when you are using the oldBlockHandling value replace.

You can use the /fill command with the destroy option to clear a large area AND get the mining drops from it. Be careful though, Minecraft has no "Undo" button.

Examples

```
/fill -480 69 180 -500 89 200 diamond_ore
/fill ~2 ~ ~2 ~12 ~-5 ~12 air 0 destroy
```

The /replaceitem Command

This command modifies inventories of chests and players. You can use it to give items to players, refill dungeon chests, or equip mobs with weapons!

Syntax

```
/replaceitem block <x> <y> <z> <slot>
<item> [amount]
```

This runs the command in block mode, which modifies chests, furnaces, and any block with an inventory.

You can also run it in entity mode, which modifies the inventories of players or mobs:

```
/replaceitem entity <selector>
<container.slot_number> <item> [amount]
```

- In block mode, replace <x>, <y>, and <z> with the coordinates of the block you want to modify.

- In entity mode, replace <selector> with the player name or target selector of the entity you want to modify

- Replace <slot_number> with the number of the inventory slot you want to replace. Slot numbers for chests start at container.0 in the top left corner and increase from left to right. Slot numbers for players are a little more complex.

  ○ For inventory slots, use container. *slot_number*, where slot_number is the number from 0 to 26 of the slot you want to modify.

- For slots on the toolbar, use hotbar.*slot_number*, where slot_number is the number from 0 to 8 of the slot you want to modify.
- For armor slots, use armor.chest, armor.head, armor.feet, and armor.legs. These don't need numbers.

- Replace <item> with the ID name of the block you are adding.

- May replace [amount] with the amount of blocks you are adding.

Examples

```
/replaceitem block ^ ^1 ^ container.0
minecraft:diamond_sword 1
```

Replace the first slot (container.0) in a chest 1 block in front of you with a new diamond sword.

```
/replaceitem entity @a container.0
minecraft:stone 64
```

Replace the first item in each players inventory with a stack of stone. Useful for building!

This command changes a specific block in the world into a different type of block.

Syntax

```
/setblock <x y z> <block>
[oldBlockHandling]
```

- Replace <x y z> with the XYZ coordinates of the block you are changing.

- Replace <TileName> with the ID name of the new block.

- May replace [oldBlockHandling] with one of the following:

    - **destroy:** This makes the old block drop as if it were mined.
    - **keep:** This will only change the block if it is an air block.
    - **replace:** This is the default.

Example

```
/setblock ~ ~-1 ~ minecraft:andesite
destroy
```

(This will change the existing block at your feet to andesite.)

CHAPTER 8

ENTITY COMMANDS

ntity commands are commands you can use on entities. Entities are moving objects in the Minecraft world, like players, mobs, minecarts, and arrows. (However, most of these entity-restricted commands do not work on vehicles or projectiles.) The reason that there are somewhat different commands for the many types of Minecraft objects is because the objects in the various categories are programmed a bit differently. They have different abilities, and entities are much more complicated than most static blocks. A wolf, for example, can be "angry" (hostile), but it can also be tamed and have a collar, and you can breed it for more wolf cubs. A dirt block is pretty much just a dirt block.

Entity commands include:

/clear
/effect
/execute
/kill

/particle
/replaceitem
/spreadplayers
/summon
/tp

The /effect Command

The /effect command lets you put status effects on entities (and remove effects from them), including players. For example, you can put the Blindness effect on any player entering a dark dungeon in a map you have made. Even if the player has torches, these won't help much. Look at Appendix E for a list of status effects.

Someone with the Blindness effect can still see, but only a few blocks around them. Even if it's daylight or there are torches, everything else is black.

Syntax

```
/effect <entity> <effect> [seconds]
[amplifier] [hideParticles]
```

- Replace <player> with a player's username or a target selector.

- Replace <effect> with the ID name for the status effect you want.

- May replace [seconds] with the time in seconds of how long the effect should last.

- May replace [amplifier] with the "strength" of the effect, from 0 (the lowest strength) to 255.

- May replace [hideParticles] with true or false (the default is "false"). Selecting "true" will hide the swirly particle effects from the status effect.

To remove effects use:

```
/effect clear <entity> [<effect>]
```

Example

```
/effect give @p minecraft:fire_resistance 12 40
false
```

The /execute Command

The /execute command is used to run commands as if another entity had run them. It can also be used to execute a command for many entities at once. /execute is a very advanced command and has many forms, parts, possible subcommands, and variables. In its simplest form, the execute command chooses another entity to serve as the executor of a command, as in the following example..

Syntax

```
/execute as <entity> run <command>
```

- Replace <entity> with an entity name or target selector.

- Replace <command> with the command you want to run.

Example

```
/execute as @r run experience add @p 120
levels
```

This will give the nearest player to a randomly selected player 120 experience levels.

The /kill Command

This is a simple command to kill (remove) any entity, including minecarts, boats, and mobs.

Syntax

`/kill [player|entity]`

- With command blocks, you must replace [player| entity] with a player's name or a target selector. With the Chat window, this is optional, and typing in just /kill will kill yourself. (This can actually be handy in Creative mode—you return to your spawn quickly. Because you are in Creative, it's easy to replace your inventory items.)

Examples

```
/kill meganfair
/kill @e[type=Zombie]
/kill @e[type=!Player]
```

The /particle Command

The /particle Command allows you to create particle effects at a specified location in the world.

Using a value higher than 1 for the speed of a mobSpell effect will create multicolored swirls.

Syntax

```
/particle <name> <x y z> <xd yd zd>
<speed> [count] [mode] [<player>]
```

- Replace <name> with the particle ID name.

- Replace <x y z> with the coordinates of the location you want the particle effect.

- Replace <xd yd zd> with size of the area to spawn the particles: how wide (along the X axis), how tall (along the Y axis), and how wide again (along the Z axis). Using 1 1 1 here will spawn the particles in a one-block cube. (However, many of these effects use a wider area, regardless.)

- Replace <speed> with a number of 0 (the lowest speed) or higher to increase the speed. Generally, the faster the speed, the shorter the time you can see the effect, so slower speeds, like 0 or 0.05 are good.

- May replace [count] with a number from 0 (1 particle) up, for the total number of particles in the effect. Watch out for really high numbers here, because that can lag or even crash Minecraft. On my PC, numbers around a million started a lag for the happy villager effect, but your mileage may vary.

- May replace [mode] with either "normal" or "force" to make the particles visible by players who have set particles to be minimal in their video options. The default is "normal."

- May replace <player> with the name of a player. This restricts who can see the effect to just the named player.

Example

```
/particle minecraft:heart ~ ~ ~ 4 4 4 0 44
normal
```

The /spreadplayers Command

This command will teleport a number of players into an area, all a certain distance from each other. Useful for spawning players in a mini-game!

Syntax

```
/spreadplayers <x> <z> <spreadDistance>
<maxRange> <respectTeams> <player...>
```

- Replace <x> and <z> with the coordinates of the center of the area you want players to teleport into.

- Replace <spreadDistance> with the minimum distance players can be from each other. Must be a positive number.

- Replace <maxRange> with the radius of the teleport area.

- Replace <respectTeams> with true or false. If you set it to true, it will group players by team. If not, it will be a free-for-all!

- Replace <player...> with one or more player names or a target selector. You can also target entities with this command.

Examples

```
/spreadplayers 0 0 1 10 false @a
```

You can summon mobs riding on top of other mobs, like this stack of slimes on top of smaller slimes.

The /summon command is a great command to play with. You can create any Minecraft entity, and even some hidden mobs you don't see in the game, like giant zombies. When you are changing things like data tags, to give a mob enchanted armor, for example, managing the brackets correctly can be hard.

Syntax

`/summon <EntityName> [x] [y] [z] [dataTag]`

- Replace <EntityName> with the entity ID name.

- May replace [x y z] with the coordinates to summon the entity to.

- May replace [dataTag] with a data tag that is appropriate for the entity.

Examples

To summon three slimes of increasing sizes, each one riding on top of the next smallest:

```
/summon slime ~ ~2 ~ {Size:3,Passengers:
[{id:slime, Size:5,Passengers:[{id:slime,
Size:7}]}]}
```

To summon a villager that will give you a diamond for each block of dirt you give him:

```
/summon villager ~1 ~ ~ {Offers:{Recipes:
[{buy:{id:dirt,Count:1},sell:{id:diamond,
Count:1},rewardExp:false}]}}
```

You can create all types of customized entities, such as this tamed zombie horse, using the /summon command.

To create a tame zombie horse with a saddle, ready to ride:

```
/summon zombie_horse ~ ~1 ~ {Tame:1,
SaddleItem:{id:saddle,Count:1}}
```

To create an overpowered zombie with 200 health points that can cause 15 points of damage:

```
/summon zombie ~0 ~1 ~0 {Attributes:
[{Name:generic.maxHealth,Base:200},
{Name:generic.attackDamage,
Base:15}],Health:200.0f}
```

Using /summon for Fireworks

You can use the /summon command to create amazing fireworks displays. Here's an example:

```
/summon firework_rocket ~ ~1 ~ {LifeTime:30,
FireworksItem:{id:firework_rocket,Count:1,
tag:{Fireworks:{Flight:2,Explosions:
[{Type:4,Flicker:1,Trail:1,Colors:
[I;14602026,15435844],FadeColors:
[I;4312372]}]}}}}
```

In addition to the entity name and the XYZ coordinates, this command uses several data tags:

- **Lifetime:** The number of seconds before the fireworks explosion

- Fireworks item {id: firework_rocket,Count:1}, which also has tags

  ○ **Flight** (distance of flight)
  ○ **Explosion** (type of explosion)
  ○ **Flicker** (true or false): for the twinkle effect
  ○ **Trail** (true or false): for the diamond trail effect

- ○ **Type**: for the shape of the explosion
- ○ **Colors**: for the color(s) the effect can be
- ○ **FadeColors**: for the colors to use as the image fades away

As you can see, nested data tags (one inside the other) make for a complicated series of brackets. And this is just one firework; you can have many inside the same command. Notice the color selection, too, uses a special format that is difficult to create. To make creating your own fireworks easier, you can use an online generator, where you can pick the shapes and colors and timing and just copy and paste the result into your own command block. One generator is at: www.minecraftupdates.com/fireworks. You can also just use a Minecraft color generator to pick your colors, like this one at https://www.digminecraft.com/generators/give_fireworks_rocket.php

The /teleport Command

The /teleport command lets you or another player or entity instantly teleport somewhere in your world. You can teleport either to wherever another player is or to a specific set of coordinates. You can use command blocks to set up a teleportation hub that has buttons to teleport you to all your favorite locations.

Syntax
To send a player to the location of another player or entity:

```
/teleport [target player] <destination
player>
```

To send a player to a specific coordinate location:

```
/teleport [target player] <x y z> [<y-rot>
<x-rot>]
```

In command blocks, you must replace [target player] with a player's name or a target selector. You will teleport yourself if you are omitting this and using the Chat window.

- Replace <destination player> with the destination player's name or a target selector.

- Replace <x y z> with the coordinates of the destination.

- May replace <y-rot> with the number of degrees of rotation horizontally (180 (to face north), -90 (east), 0 (south), 90 (west)) and <x-rot> with the number of degrees of vertical rotation (90 is facing down, -90 is facing up).

Examples

```
/teleport meganfair cappymiller
/teleport meganfair ~10 ~ ~10 180 90
```

CHAPTER 9

PLAYER COMMANDS

Player commands work on target players. Players are a type of entity in the game programming, so you can use most entity commands on players as well. However, you can't use all player commands on entities, because not all entities are players! There are some great player commands: /give lets you give any item to a player, including weapons enchanted with higher levels than possible in the regular game.

Player commands include:

/advancement
/enchant
/experience
/give
/playsound
/spawnpoint

The /advancement Command

This command lets you give (grant) or take away (revoke) advancements to a player. Advancements and custom advancements can be used in creating minigames and maps. For example, you could reward a player who reached a difficult goal on your map by giving them all advancements. Every advancement includes one or more actions (criterion) that have to be performed by the player in order to get that advancement.

Syntax

```
/advancement   <grant|revoke> <player>
only|until|from|through <advancement>
[criterion]
```

```
/advancement   <grant|revoke> <player>
everything
```

- Choose **grant** if you wish to give advancements or revoke for removing advancements.

- Replace *<player>* with the name of a player or a target selector.

- Choose **only** if you are granting/revoking just one advancement. Choose **until** to grant the advancement and all advancements that lead to that advancement (parents). Choose **from** to select the advancement as well as any following (children) advancements. Choose **through** to select an advancement and both parent and children advancements.

- Replace *<advancement>* with the ID for the advancement you are granting/revoking.

- Can replace [criterion] with one of the criterion(s) used for an advancement. The syntax for advancement criterion and programming is beyond the scope of this book but you can find out more about this at the Minecraft Wiki.

- Choose **everything**, using the second syntax, to grant/revoke all advancements to a player.

The /enchant Command

With the /enchant command, you can enchant armor, weapons, and tools. You can only enchant one item at a time, and the item has to be in the player's hand (selected in his or her inventory). You have to stick to enchantments that are possible in the regular game though, so you can't enchant a sword with Sharpness X (10). To give a custom enchantment like that, use the /give command.

Syntax

```
/enchant <player> <enchantment ID> [level]
```

- Replace <player> with a player's name or target selector.

- Replace <enchantment ID> with the enchantment's ID name (See Appendix D for a list of enchantment IDs.)

- May replace [level] with the level of enchantment. The limit is 5, 4, 3, or 1 for many enchantments. While the enchantments in the game use Roman numerals (like Sharpness III), here you use a regular numeral (like 1 or 3) for the level.

Example

```
/enchant cappymiller minecraft:sharpness 2
```

The /experience Command

The /experience command lets you give XP points or XP levels to any player.

Syntax

```
/experience <add|set|query> <player>
<amount> [points|levels]
```

```
/experience
```

- Choose "add" to add experience or "set" to change the player's experience level to a specific amount. Choose query to have the command return the amount of experience they have. With this option, you don't use <amount>. Replace <amount> with the number of points or levels of XP you are giving.

- Must replace [player] with a player name or target selector if you are using command blocks. Otherwise this is optional, and if you omit it, then you will get the XP points or levels.

- Replace <amount> with the number of experience points or levels that you are adding.

- Choose points or levels to specify the measure of experience you want to use.

Examples

```
/experience 30L @p
/experience 300 meganfair
```

The /give Command

The /give command lets you give any Minecraft item or block to a player. Because you can use data tags to modify the item you are giving, you can use this command to give items that are enchanted to a higher level than possible in the game.

Syntax

```
/give <player> <item>[<dataTag>] [amount]
```

- Replace <player> with a player's name or a target selector.

- Replace <item> with the block ID name or item ID name you are giving.

- May replace [dataTag] with a valid data tag for the item.

- May replace [amount] with the number of the item you want to give.

With the /give command, you can give items that are enchanted with levels much higher than allowed in the game.

Examples

```
/give @a cookie 10 0
/give MegorniusPI golden_apple 1 0
{display:{Name:Apple O Life}}

/give @p golden_sword 1 0 {ench:[{id:16,lvl 7},
{id:20,lvl:5},{id:19,lvl:5}],display:
{Name:"Creepa Killa",Lore:[Burn Creepers
and Hurl Them!]}}
```

The /playsound Command

With the /playsound command, you can play one of the sounds in Minecraft to another player. For example, if you have a command block with a particle effect of an explosion going off at a fort, you could add a sound effect of the explosion with another command block. You can find a list of these sounds on the Minecraft Wiki at http://minecraft.gamepedia.com/Sounds.json#Sound_events. Some of these sound events have several different sounds that are played randomly. For example, a ghast has seven different moaning sounds, all associated with the sound event mob.ghast.moan.

Syntax

```
/playsound <sound> <source> <player> [x y z]
[volume] [pitch] [minimumVolume]
```

- Replace <sound> with the name of the Minecraft sound event.

- Replace <source> with the source category the sound will play from, to, such as "weather", "music", etc.

- Replace <player> with a player's name or a target selector.

- May replace <x y z> with the location for the origin of the sound.

- May replace [volume] with a number from 0.0 up. The default is 1.0. Numbers under 1.0 are quieter and don't carry as far. For numbers above the 1.0 range, the sound carries farther.

- May replace [pitch] with a number between 0.0 and 2.0 that raises or lowers the pitch. 1.0 is the default, and numbers below this lower the pitch. Numbers above this raise the pitch.

- May replace [minimumVolume] with a number between 0.0 and 1.0 to represent how loud the sound is for players that aren't within the normal range for the sound.

Examples

```
/playsound minecraft:block.ender_chest.open
block cappymiller
/playsound minecraft:entity.blaze.ambient
voice @a
```

Minecraft has a long list of sounds you can play with the /playsound command, including the sound of a player burping while they eat.

The /spawnpoint Command

With /spawnpoint you can set your or another player's spawn point in the world.

Syntax

`/spawnpoint [player] [x y z]`

- Must replace [player] with a player's name or a target selector if you are using command blocks. If not, you can omit this and the command will change your own spawn point.

- May replace [x y z] with the coordinates for the new spawn point. If you don't include this, the spawn point will be wherever the command is issued.

Examples

```
/spawnpoint @p ~ ~ ~
/spawnpoint cappymiller 500 64 -345
```

APPENDIX A

BLOCK , ITEM, AND ENTITY ID NAMES

Minecraft blocks and items are the things you place, use, wear, or hold in Minecraft. Although most blocks take up the full block space, some don't, like brewing stands. All blocks can be placed, while items are objects you use, like swords. Entities, in general, are those elements that move around or have special functions: like players, villagers, mobs, and projectiles.

Minecraft used to use ID numbers to help identify items, but it now uses ID names. Almost all of these ID names are simply lowercased versions of the item's in-game name, using an underscore in place of spaces. For example, the ID name for a heavy weighted pressure plate is heavy_weighted_pressure_plate. The ID name for a Zombie Pigman is zombie_pigman. Minecraft's autocomplete feature will help you find the correct name, but if you are using a third party program to plan out complicated commands, it can help to know how to figure out the official ID name. You can also view the ID name lists on the Minecraft Wiki at https://minecraft.gamepedia.com/Java_Edition_data_values or you can search for other compiled lists of names online by searching for Minecraft ID names.

Translating the In Game Names to ID Names

This works for most blocks.

(1) For single word names, simply lowercase the name: **stone**, **dirt**, **cobweb**.

(2) For multiple word names: use lowercase as well and replace spaces between the words with an underscore: **birch_planks**; **stripped_dark_oak_log**, **purple_carpet**, **red_terracotta**, **pink_wool**

Exceptions

There are a few blocks/items/entities currently that don't quite fit these rules:

Block of Diamond	diamond_block
Block of Emerald	emerald_block
Block of Gold	gold_block
Block of Iron	iron_block
Block of Quartz	quartz_block
Block of Redstone	redstone_block
Book and Quill	writable_book
Bottle o' Enchanting	experience_bottle
Bucket of [fishname]	pufferfish_bucket, salmon_bucket, cod_bucket, tropical_fish_bucket
clay	clay_ball
Dragon's Breath	dragon_breath
Eye of Ender	ender_eye
Hay Bale	hay_block
Jack o'Lantern	jack_o_lantern

Lapis Lazuli Block	lapis_block
Lapis Lazuli Ore	lapis_ore
Leather Cap	leather_helmet
Leather Pants	leather_leggins
Leather Tunic	leather_chestplate
Map or Explorer Map	filled_map
Minecart with Chest	chest_minecart
Minecart with Command Block	command_block_minecart
Minecart with furnace	furnace_minecart
Minecart with Spawner	spawner_minecart
Minecart with TNT	tnt_minecart
Rabbit's Foot	rabbit_foot
Raw Beef	beef
Raw Mutton	mutton
Redstone Comparator	comparator
Redstone Dust	redstone_wire
Redstone Repeater	repeater
Slimeball	slime_ball
Steak	cooked_beef
Turtle Shell	turtle_helmet
Vines	vine

POTION TAGS

To give a potion, you must use the item ID Potion along with the appropriate data tags to specify the potion you want. For example, to give everyone two slowness potions, you type:

```
/give @a potion{Potion:slowness} 2
```

To give these as splash potions, use

```
/give @a splash_potion{Potion:slowness}
```

The values for standard potions are listed below. To specify a Level II potion (if allowed), add **strong_** before the potion value, as in **strong_leaping.** To specify an extended length potion, add **long_** before the name, as in **long_turtle_master**.

Awkward Potion	awkward
Fire Resistance	fire_resistance, long_fire_resistance
Harming	harming, strong_harming
Instant Health	healing, strong_healing
Invisibility	invisibility, long_invisibility
Leaping	leaping, strong_leaping, long_leaping
Luck	luck
Mundane Potion	mundane
Night Vision	night_vision, long_night_vision
Poison	poison, strong_poison, long_poison
Regeneration	regeneration, strong_regeneration, long_regeneration
Slow Falling	slow_falling, long_slow_falling
Slowness	slowness, strong_slowness, long_slowness
Strength	strength, strong_strength, long strength
Swiftness	swiftness, strong_swiftness, long_swiftness
The Turtle Master	turtle_master, strong_turtle_master, long_turtle_master
Thick Potion	thick
Water Bottle	water
Water Breathing	water_breathing, long_water_breathing
Weakness	weakness, long_weakness

ENCHANTMENT IDs

These IDs are used with the /give command and the /enchant command. The Highest Level is the maximum level the enchantment can have in regular gameplay.

Enchantment	Name	Highest Legitimate Level
Aqua Affinity	aqua_affinity	1
Bane of Arthropods	bane_of_arthropods	5
Blast Protection	blast_protection	4

Channeling	channeling	1
Curse of Binding	binding_curse	1
Curse of Vanishing	Vanishing_curse	1
Depth Strider	depth_strider	3
Efficiency	efficiency	5
Feather Falling	feather_falling	4
Fire Aspect	fire_aspect	2
Fire Protection	fire_protection	4
Flame	flame	1
Fortune	fortune	3
Frost Walker	frost_walker	2
Impaling	Impaling	5
Infinity	infinity	1
Knockback	knockback	2
Looting	looting	3
Loyalty	loyalty	3
Luck of the Sea	luck_of_the_sea	3
Lure	lure	3
Mending	mending	1
Power	power	5
Projectile Protection	projectile_protection	4
Protection	protection	4
Punch	punch	2

Respiration	respiration	3
Riptide	riptide	3
Sharpness	sharpness	5
Silk Touch	silk_touch	1
Smite	smite	5
Sweeping Edge	sweeping	3
Thorns	thorns	3
Unbreaking	unbreaking	3

STATUS EFFECTS

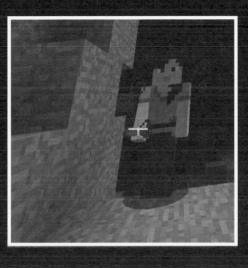

Use these ID names for status effects with the /effect command.

	Status Effect	ID Name
💜	Absorption	absorption
🍀	Bad Luck	unluck
👁	Blindness	blindness
🔵	Conduit Power	conduit_power

	Dolphin's Grace	dolphins_grace
	Fire Resistance	fire_resistance
	Glowing	glowing
	Haste	haste
	Health Boost	health_boost
	Hunger	hunger
−	Instant Damage	instant_damage
−	Instant Health	instant_health
	Invisibility	invisibility
	Jump Boost	jump_boost
	Levitation	levitation
	Luck	luck
	Mining Fatigue	mining_fatigue
	Nausea	nausea
	Night Vision	night_vision
	Poison	poison
	Regeneration	regeneration

	Resistance	resistance
	Saturation	saturation
	Slow Falling	slow_falling
	Slowness	slowness
	Speed	speed
	Strength	strength
	Water Breathing	water_breathing
	Weakness	weakness
	Wither	wither

PARTICLES

se these ID names for visual effects with the /particle command.

This is a shortened version of the full particle list at the Minecraft Wiki. For the full list, visit minecraft.gamepedia.com/Particles

angryVillager
bubble (only works
  underwater)
cloud
crit

dripping_water
dripping_lava
dragon_breath
effect
enchant

enchanted_hit

explosion

explosion_emitter

falling_dust

firework

fishing

flame

happy_villager

heart

hugeexplosion

instant_effect

item_slime

item_snowball

lava

note

poof

portal

rain

reddust

smoke

spit

splash

squid_ink

underwater

witch

COMMANDS

This list covers most Minecraft commands, but not server administration commands. To learn more about commands that manage a server, visit the Minecraft Wiki at minecraft. gamepedia.com/Commands.

Italics show the text that must be replaced. The angle brackets show parameters that must be included, and the square brackets show optional parameters. (These brackets shouldn't be included in the command.) Also, the commands and syntax below start with a slash. The slash is required for commands used in the Chat window but optional for commands used in a command block.

Command	Syntax
/advancement	/advancement <grant|revoke> <*player*> only <*advancement*> [*criterion*] /advancement <grant|revoke> <*player*> <until|from|through> <*advancement*> /advancement <grant|revoke> <*player*> everything
/bossbar	/bossbar add <id> <player> /bossbar set <id> (name|col or|style|value|max|players) <name|color|style|value|max| visible|players> /bossbar set <id> value /bossbar remove <id> /bossbar list /bossbar get <id> (max|players|value|visible) (Note: styles are notched_6, notched_10, notched_12, and progress (default); visible may be true/false)

Command	Syntax
/data	`/data get block <pos> [<path>] [<scale>]`
	`/data get entity <target> [<path>] [<scale>]`
	`/data merge block <pos> <nbt>`
	`/data merge entity <target> <nbt>`
	`/data remove block <pos> <path>`
	`/data remove entity <target> <path>`
/datapack	`/datapack disable <name>`
	`/datapack enable <name> [first|last]`
	`/datapack enable <name> [before|after] <existing>`
	`/datapack list [available|enabled]`
/experience	`/experience add <players> <amount> [points|levels]`
	`/experience set <players> <amount> [points|levels]`
	`/experience query <player> <points|levels>`
/locate	`/locate <StructureType>`

Command	Syntax
/recipe	`/recipe <give|take> [player] <name|*>`

/teleport	`/teleport <destination>`
	
	`/teleport <player> <destination>`
	
	`/teleport <player> <entity>`
	
	`/teleport <player> <location> facing <facingLocation>`
	
	`/teleport <player> <location> facing entity <facingEntity> [<facingAnchor>]`
	
	`/teleport <player> <location> [<rotation>]`

*Source: Minecraft Wiki at minecraft.gamepedia.com/Commands and the Minecraft Java Edition 1.13.